THE SCHOOLKIDS' JOKE BOOK 2000

Also by Brough Girling and Tony Blundell:

The Schoolkids' Joke Book
The Schoolkids' Joke Book Too!

and in the Jets series:

Clever Trevor
Nora Bone
Nora Bone and the Tooth Fairy
The Mystery of Lydia Dustbin's Diary

Compiled by Brough Girling
Illustrated by Tony Blundell

An imprint of HarperCollins*Publishers*

First published in Great Britain in hardback by Collins in 2000
Collins is an imprint of HarperCollins*Publishers* Ltd
77-85 Fulham Palace Road, Hammersmith, London W6 8JB

1 3 5 7 9 8 6 4 2

ISBN 0 00 694603 8

Printed and bound in Great Britain by
Omnia Books Limited, Glasgow

**For details of Readathon write to:
Readathon, Swerford, Chipping Norton, OX7 4BG
or telephone 01608 730335**

FOREWORD

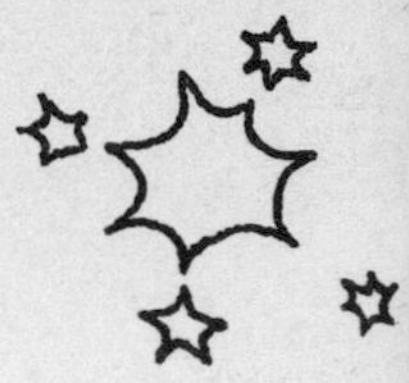

What's the difference between an onion and a joke book?
Nobody cries if you chop up a joke book!

Well, that's what Oliver Gale-Grant from The Mall School in Twickenham thinks. He was just one of the hundreds of school kids who sent in jokes for this new, *bumperjoketastic* collection of side-splitters!

All these joke senders have one thing in common – apart from their taste in gigglesome ghastliness. They have taken part in ***Readathon***, the national sponsored reading event that raises over a million pounds every year for very ill children. So well done to them for that, and for sending in some of the playground's daisyfreshest new jokes, as well as lots of the world's oldest. Many thanks to all their teachers too!

A few of the *very* oldest jokes can be found in a special section called Old Chestnuts on Page 90. But the newest and best have received **NEW CHESTNUT AWARDS**! These are no doubt destined to become future classics.

Brough Girling

FAVOURITE JOKES!

Everyone's got a favourite joke, but these jokes are all about ***favourites***!

What's a penguin's favourite party game?
Sardines!
Naresh Selopal

What's a dragon's favourite party game?
Swallow my leader!
David Jones

What's a school cleaner's
favourite fairy tale?
Sweeping Beauty!
Robert Boswell

What is a cow's favourite holiday destination?
Moo Zealand!
Hannah Brown

Or maybe Moo York!
Laura Jenks

What is a bee's favourite holiday destination?
Stingapore!
William Dalleywater

What's a cat's favourite Sunday newspaper?
Mews of the World!
Laura Fletcher

What's a duck's favourite biscuit?
Queam Quackers!
Robert Boswell

What's a space traveller's favourite game?
Astronoughts and crosses!
Subhraj Sidhu

What's a snail's favourite brand of petrol?
Shell!
Thomas Spring

What's a vampire's favourite fruit?
Blood orange!
P Parker

What's a horse's favourite game?
Stable tennis!
Nicola Lloyd

What's a cat's favourite dessert?
Mice pudding!
Henry Fields

What's a skeleton's favourite shellfish?
Mussels!
Robert Boswell

What was Dracula's favourite game?
Batminton!
Charlie Kenber

ANIMAL CRACKERS!

There's no doubt about it, school kids think animals are the funniest thing on the planet (except for teachers of course).

What's the difference between an elephant and a biscuit?
You wouldn't want to dunk an elephant in your tea!
Britta Ney

What time is it when an elephant sits on your fence?
Time to get a new fence!
James Maisey

NEW CHESTNUT AWARD!

A baby camel says to its mum, "Mum, what are our humps for?"

Mum says, "to store water so that we don't need a drink when we trek across the desert."

"So why have we got enormous feet?" asks the baby camel.

"To stop us sinking into the sand in the desert."

Baby camel says, "so what are we doing here in Newquay Zoo?"
Catherine White

What do you call a duck that swims in cream?
A cream quacker!
Kate Newman

What do you call a Rottweiler with a machine gun?
Sir!
James Adams

Bulldog for sale – will eat anything – very fond of children.
Conor Cairns

Where does a three metre eagle sleep?
Anywhere it wants to!
Alex Thomas

What do female sheep wear?
Eweniforms!
Chelsea Evans

What do you do if you see a blue elephant?
Try and cheer it up!
Chelsea Evans

Incidentally, a blue elephant is called a Glumbo!
Stacey Reid

Why are elephants wrinkled?
Have you ever tried to iron one?!
Catherine White

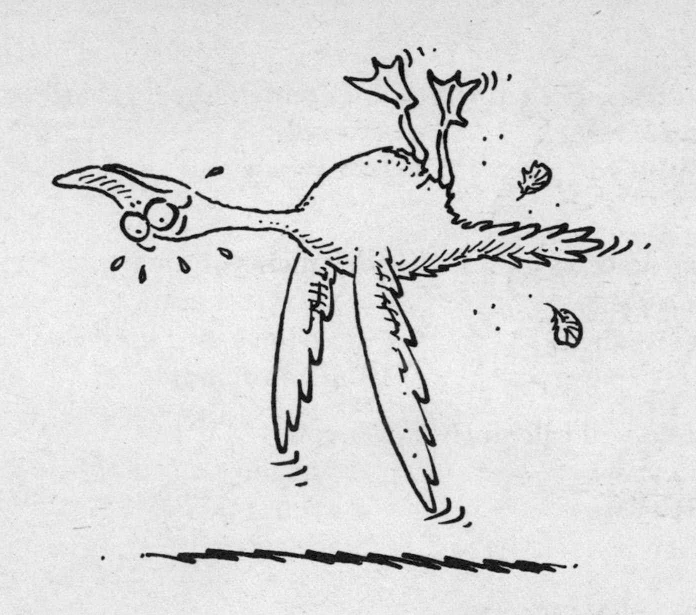

What happens when ducks fly upside down?
They quack up!
Samantha Rutherford

When should a mouse carry an umbrella?
When it's raining cats and dogs!
Conor Cairns

A horse walks into a bar and orders a large coke.
"OK" says the barman, "but why the long face?"
Catherine White

Why do giraffes have such long legs?
Because they've got smelly feet!
Luke Jones

How do sheep keep warm?
Central bleating!
Laura Lloyd

Where do cows go on Saturday nights?
The moovies!
Emily Redhead

What do you call an Eskimo's cow?
An Eskimoo!
Monty Cann

What do you call a bird that wears a shell suit?
An egg!
Amy Baker

What do giraffes have that no other animals have?
Baby giraffes!
Katherine Wells

Baby snake: Are we poisonous, Mum?
Mummy snake: Yes dear.
Baby snake: Oh no! I've just bitten my lip!
Andrew Iacovides

What lion doesn't roar?
A dandylion!
Billy Gardiner

What do you give an ill frog?
A hoperation!
Rachael McKnight

What bird is always out of breath?
A Puffin!
Meera Mistry

Why do swallows fly south in the winter?
It's too far to walk!
Katherine Wells

What's the smallest ant in the world?
An infant!
Meera Mistry

What is the fastest fish in the sea?
A motor pike!
Sara Tidey

GHASTLY GAGS

All these jokes have Parental Guidance certificates – so don't let your mum or dad see them!

NEW CHESTNUT AWARD!

Seen on the back of a biker's jacket:
If you can read this, my wife has fallen off!
Penny Johnson

A gang of vampires broke into a blood bank and stole a thousand pints of blood.
Police are still hunting for the clots.
Jenny Roffe

Two lions were eating a clown and one says to the other: "Doesn't this meat taste funny!"
Jo Carpenter

Man: How much are those puppies in the window?
Pet Shop Owner: They're thirty pounds apiece.
Man: How much is a whole one?
Eddy Turner

What's the difference between school dinners and horse poo?
School dinners are normally cold!
Jenelle Corry

What happened to the boy who drank eight cans of fizzy drink?
He brought 7 up!
Joseph Cooper

Why did Tigger look down the toilet?
To find Pooh!
Rachael Golden

Why did the hedgehog cross the road?
To show he had guts!
Gemma Evans

What goes Baa—
aaa-aaaa-aaa!?
A sheep falling off a cliff!
Theo Acworth

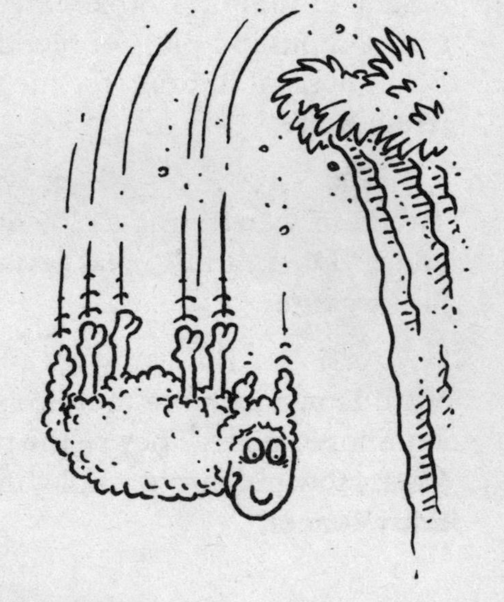

What's green, round and smells?
Kermit's bottom!
Sarah Jones

What's yellow and smells of bananas?
Monkey sick!
Gemma Evans

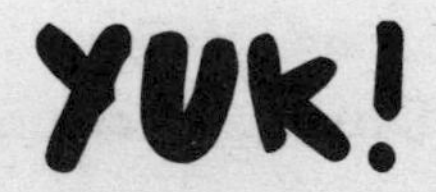

CROSSES!

Don't get cross – they're only jokes!

What do you get if you cross a dog with a row of mountains?
A Range Rover!
Sam Waghorn

What do you get if you cross a kangaroo with a sheep and a crocodile?
A snappy woolly jumper!
Jade Dymond

What do you get if you cross an ice cream with a football team?
Aston Vanilla!
Duncan McCombe

What do you get if you cross a centipede with a parrot?
A walkie talkie!
Sara Tidey

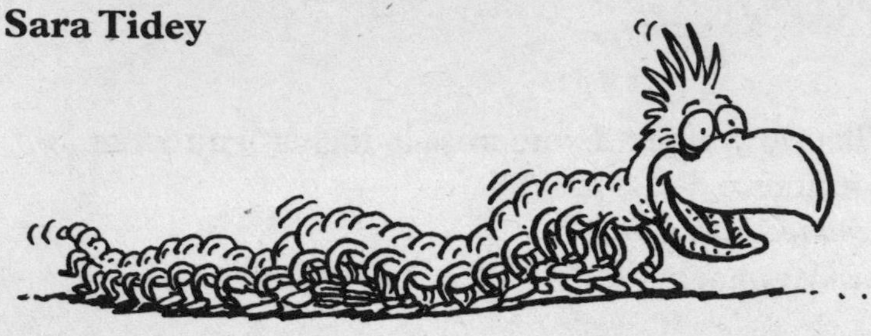

What do you get if you cross an opera with a computer?
Turandot.com!
Roger Judd

What do you get if you cross a fish with an elephant?
Swimming trunks!
Duncan McCombe

What do you get if you cross naked people with a Scottish newspaper?
Och Aye the Nudes!
Robert Swaine

What do you get if you cross a turkey with a banjo?
A bird that plucks itself!
Louise McCullock

What do you get if you cross a duck with a cracker?
A Christmas quacker!
Jennifer O'Hare

What do you get if you cross Dracula with snow?
Frostbite!
Charles Harrison

What do you get if you cross a pig with a zebra?
Striped sausages!
Joseph Stevenson

What do you get if you cross a bird with a sheep?
A cheep baagain!
Jemma Padden

CLEVERCLOGS' CORNER

The kids who sent these in are bound to get lots of Ho Ho levels…
(or even G.C. Tee Hees!)

Bacteria: the rear entrance to a cafeteria.
Namir Kubba

What are nitrates?
I don't know, but I expect they're cheaper than day rates!
Namir Kubba

A taxi driver was going the wrong way down a one-way street. He went past a policeman who ignored him. Why?
He was walking!
J Patel

What stands in the middle of Paris?
The letter R.
Maurits Pat

What is full of holes, but can hold water?
A sponge!
Kieran Colaco

Why are there fouls in football?
Because there are ducks in cricket!
Joseph Stevenson

Why is Europe like a cooking pot?
Because it's got Turkey in it and Greece on the bottom!
Emily Diamond

Teacher: Why did Tchaikovsky write this piece in four flats?
Boy: He had to keep moving because he couldn't pay the rent!
Haig Agulian

If two is company, and three is a crowd, what's four and five?
Nine!
Chelsea Evans

If the red house was made out of red bricks, and the blue house was made out of blue bricks, what was the green house made out of?
Glass!
Oliver Cotes-James

What is the best way to make a fire using two sticks?
Make sure at least one of them is a match!
Katherine Wells

A man rides into town on Friday, stays three nights and leaves on Saturday morning.
How is this possible?
His horse was called Friday!
J Patel

What can a whole apple do that half an apple can't?
Look round!
Anna Heathorn

Where is Hadrian's Wall?
At the bottom of Hadrian's garden!
Amar Winayat

NEW CHESTNUT AWARD!

Why did the French man only have one egg for breakfast?
Because un oeuf is un oeuf!
William Thomas

There was a red bungalow. Everything in it was red – the walls, the carpets, the furniture.
What colour were the stairs?
There weren't any: it was a bungalow!
Hugo Walford

Why did the – cross the road?
Because it + to!
Rosemary Hurford

Why is 6 afraid of 7?
Because 7, 8, 9!
Charles Harrison

What's the longest word in English?
SMILES – because there's a mile between the first and last letters!
Charlie Kenber

When Gazza was injured in the FA Cup final, who came on for him?
The St John's Ambulance Brigade!
Michael Rae

At a family reunion one man went up to another and said, "Father!"
The other man said, "Grandad!" Neither was wrong. Why?
The first man was a priest.
J Patel

PULL THE OTHER ONE

Why can't you tell a snake a joke?
Because you can't pull its leg!
And like a snake, these jokes are completely 'armless!

A refuse collector went to the back of a country mansion but he couldn't find the dustbin. He went to the front, but he couldn't find it there either. He knocked on the door and the posh owner opened it.
"Where's your bin?" asked the refuse collector.
"I've been away on holiday," said the house owner.
"No', said the refuse collector, "where's your wheely bin?"
"I've really been away" said the house owner!
Daniel Cutler

Two snails robbed a tortoise. The police asked the tortoise what happened.
"I don't know," said the tortoise, "it all happened so quickly!"
Richard Bellerby

A policeman caught two boys, one was eating fireworks and the other was drinking battery water.
One was let off, and the other was charged.
Janie Smith

Did you hear about the man who tried to iron his curtains?
He fell out of the window!
Hannah Taylor

A woman went into a pet shop and said to the owner, "Can I have a fluffy little bunny for my daughter?"
"Sorry," said the owner, "we don't do swaps!"
Richard Bellerby

At a school nativity play the three wise men came on to the stage. The first wise man put an envelope down in front of the crib. "Jonny!" said the teacher, "aren't you meant to give the baby gold?"
"Yes Miss," said Jonny, "but this is a Man United season ticket – my dad says they're just like gold!"
Luke Seward

A man took his dog to the vet. The vet told him that unfortunately the dog was very ill.

"I want a second opinion," said the man.

So the vet asked a cat who was in the room, and the cat miaowed.

"There," said the vet, "the cat agrees with me."

"Well I still want another opinion," said the man.

The vet asked a large Labrador.

"Woof!" said the Labrador.

"There you are," said the vet, "the Labrador agrees with me too."

"OK!" said the man. "How much do I owe you?"

"£600," said the vet.

"What?! That's an awful lot!"

"Yes," said the vet, "but you've had my opinion, and a cat scan, and a lab test!"

Peter Knight

Did you hear about the wooden car?
It wooden go!
Kirsty Holmes

A man walks into a butcher's shop and asks the butcher, "Are you a gambling man?"
"I am," replies the butcher.
"OK," says the man, "I bet you can't jump up and touch that meat hanging on that hook."
"I'm not doing that," said the butcher.
"I thought you said you were a gambling man?"
"I am, but the steaks are too high!"
Nigel Fordham

A man rang up Sheffield Wednesday football ground and asked when the match on Saturday would start.
"Just bring your boots and we'll start when you're ready!" was the reply.
James Senior

There was once a very well-behaved boy. Whenever he was good his father gave him 10p and a pat on the head. By the time he was eighteen he had £780, and a flat head!

Edward Emmett

KNOCK! KNOCK!

Jokes about people who haven't got door bells...

Knock! Knock!
Who's there?
Doris.
Doris who?
Doris locked, that's why I had to knock!
Adam Chen

Knock! Knock!
Who's there?
Chris.
Chris who?
Christmas time, mistletoe and wine...
Alice Craig

Knock! Knock!
Who's there?
A titch.
A titch who?
Bless you!
Anthony Beck

Knock! Knock!
Who's there?
Boo.
Boo who?
No need to cry, it's only a joke!
Sophia Sussex

Knock! Knock!
Who's there?
Scot.
Scot who?
Scot nothing to do with you!
Lauren Syme

Knock! Knock!
Who's there?
Cook.
Cook who?
Stop making bird
noises and open
the door!
Dom Morgan

Knock! Knock!
Who's there?
Lettuce.
Lettuce who?
Lettuce in and I'll tell you!
Caroline Major

Knock! Knock!
Who's there?
Abyssinia.
Abyssinia who?
Abyssinia soon!
Jade Puckey

Knock! Knock!
Who's there?
Aunt.
Aunt who?
Aunt these jokes terrible! [Ed: YES!]
Jodie Rees

Knock! Knock!
Who's there?
Luke.
Luke who?
Luke through the keyhole and you'll see!
Jane Frost

Knock! Knock!
Who's there?
Cornflakes.
Corn Flakes who?
I'll tell you next week, it's a cereal!
Tom Hunter

Knock! Knock!
Who's there?
Phyllis.
Phyllis who?
Phyllis a glass of water, I'm thirsty!
Aaron Ireland

RIOTOUS RIDDLES

Why do school children know so many jokes? It's an absolute riddle!

What did the moon say to Saturn?
You must give me a ring sometime!
Naomi Carpenter

What goes up when the rain comes down?
Umbrellas!
Katherine Wells

Why are lawyers good tennis players?
Because they spend a lot of time in court!
Jade Puckey

What's small, round, white
and giggles?
A tickled onion!
Thomas Woodhouse

Why did the orange cross
the road?
To play squash?
No, because the peelers were after him!
Stacey Orr

What's French, very tall and makes a loud bang?
The rifle tower!
Namir Kubba

How far can a pirate ship go?
About twenty-five miles to the galleon!
Katie Sparks

What's brown and hairy and sneezes?
A coconut with a cold!
Gemma Evans

Where do baby apes sleep?
Apricots!
Jessica May

What do golfers wear?
Tee shirts!
Tom Wendland

How many ears does Captain Kirk have?
Three; a left ear, a right ear and a final front ear!
Henry Kingston

What's the fastest vegetable?
A runner bean!
Amelia Churchill Blackie

When can you see flying saucers?
When a waiter trips up!
Tom Wendland

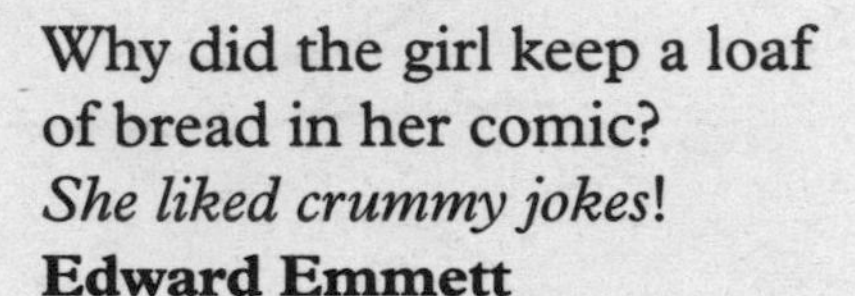

Why did the girl keep a loaf
of bread in her comic?
She liked crummy jokes!
Edward Emmett

What's the food with the worst manners?
Sausages, because they spit!
Michael Evans

What music do composers write in the bath?
Soap operas!
Sanjit Chohan

Or Handel's Water Music!
Namir Kubba

What's the difference between a nail and
a bad boxer?
One is knocked in, the other is knocked out!
H Ahluwalia

What exams do farmers take?
Hay levels!
Edward Emmett

What's round and bad-tempered?
A vicious circle!
William Dawes

What tongue can't taste?
The tongue in your shoe!
Chelsea Evans

Why does Santa come down chimneys?
Because it soots him!
David Walsh

What's the difference between a fireman and a soldier?
You can't dip a fireman in your egg!
Amelia Churchill Blackie

Why is a tomato round and red?
Because if it was long and green it would be a cucumber!
Natasha Godfrey

Why are adults boring?
Because they are groan-ups!
Meera Mistry

What's the best thing to put in a pie?
Your teeth!
Richard Bellerby

Why did the fly fly?
Because the spider spied her!
Lauren Syme

Why did the muddy chicken cross the road twice?
Because it was a dirty double crosser!
Martin Blaney

What would happen if pigs could fly?
Bacon would go up!
John Jones

Where did the snowmen dance?
At the snow ball!
Connor McCann

And why did the owl 'owl?
Because the woodpecker would peck 'er!
Tom Lee

If you drop a white hat into the red sea, what will it become?
Wet!
Katherine Wells

What house weighs the least?
A lighthouse!
Meera Mistry

How do you start a pudding race?
Sago!
H Bourden

Why should you ask a barber for directions?
They know all the short cuts!
Thomas Woodhouse

Why was the cowboy always in trouble?
Because he was always horsing around!
Luke Jones

Why is a tree noisy?
Because of its bark!
Katy Connel

NEW CHESTNUT AWARD!

What film might have been created by the author of *Charlie and the Chocolate Factory*?
101 Dahl-mations!
Andrew Iacovides

What did the jack say to the car?
Can I give you a lift?
Jenny Higson

What's purple with orange spots, has huge teeth and twelve hairy legs?
I don't know, why?
Because one's just crawled down your collar!
Charlotte White

What do you give a sick lemon?
Lemon-aid!
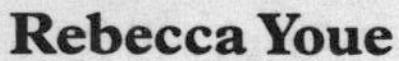
Rebecca Youe

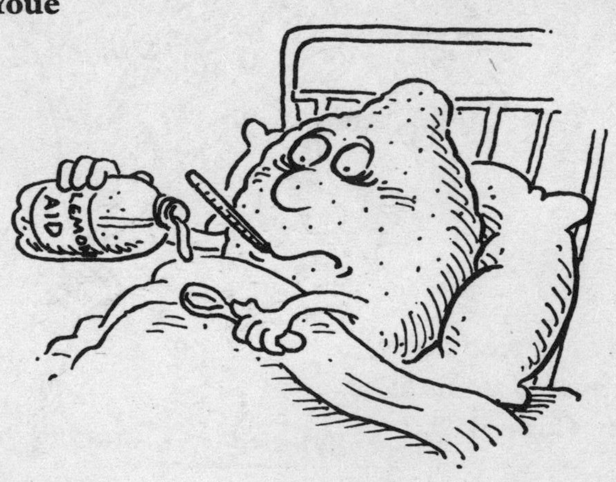

What's purple and hums?
An electric plum!
Rachel Wood

Where does a policeman live?
999 Letsby Avenue!
Laura Reaney

What's Rupert the Bear's middle name?
THE!
Simon O'Malley

GHASTLY GHOSTS AND MIRTHFUL MONSTERS!

Some jokes are an absolute scream!

What does a hungry ghost want?
Ice scream!
Victoria Sussex

What do monsters call human beings?
Breakfast, lunch and dinner!
Lauren Syme

What do vampires suck when they're ill?
Coffin drops!
Swarnjit Chohan

Why couldn't the young witch do her homework properly?
Because she couldn't spell!
Samantha Rutherford

Did you hear about the stupid ghost?
He climbed over walls!
Robert Boswell

Why did the monster eat a sofa and two chairs?
He had a suite tooth!
Andrew Iacovides

A vampire's school report
English: Good
Maths: Good
Cricket: Shows promise as a bat
Don Stuart

Who did Dracula marry?
His ghoul friend!
Joseph Stevenson

What position do ghosts play at football?
Ghoulie!
Samantha Rutherford

How do you make a witch itch?
Take away her w!
Robert Boswell

Where do ghosts go swimming?
The Dead Sea!
Swarnjit Chohan

How do ghosts travel abroad?
British Scareways!
Aaron Thompson

EVEN MORE RIDICULOUS, RIOTOUS RIDDLES!

Why couldn't the pianist open the piano?
The keys were on the inside!
Nishe Selopal

What do you give a sick bird?
Tweetment!
Sam Taberer

What's white and goes up?
A confused snowflake!
Celia Kindersley

What has a head and a tail but no body?
A coin!
Amelia Churchill Blackie

How do you start a flea market?
You start from scratch!
Sophie Cooper

What do you call James bond in the bath?
Bubble 07!
Gemma Atkins

Why did the skeleton cross the road?
To get to the Body Shop!
Caroline Banham

What does Tarzan sing at Christmas?
Jungle bells!
Zachary Grant

Why was the football pitch flooded?
Because the players had dribbled too much!
James Lambert

At least the manager could put his sub on!
Jimmy Short

What walks on its head all day?
A drawing pin stuck in your shoe!
Victoria Jones

How do you make an apple puff?
Chase it round the kitchen!
Hannah Hughes

Who is king of the tissues?
Hanky chief!
Duncan McCombe

How did Noah light the ark?
Floodlights!
Alice Woodyat

Why is a river rich?
Because it has two banks!
Aisling O'Connor

Why do soldiers wear khaki braces?
To keep their trousers up!
Katherine Wells

What do you call an old snowman?
Water!
Alan Reeve

What do you sing at a snowman's birthday party?
Freeze a jolly good fellow!
Laura Grundy

Why is there so little honey in Rio de Janeiro?
Because there's only one bee in Brazil!
Mr J P Carnegie

When is a car not a car?
When it turns into a garage!
Robert Boswell

When is it bad luck to see a black cat?
When you're a mouse!
Charlie Hope

What do you call a jacket that's on fire?
A blazer.
Duncan McCombe

What do you lose every time you stand up?
Your lap!
[And your seat, if you're on a busy train!]
Katherine Wells

Where do you find hippies?
At the top of your leggies!
Jasneel Gill

NEW CHESTNUT AWARD!

Why did the teenagers cross the road?
Because their parents told them not to!
Charlotte Thorne

What's brown and sneaks round the kitchen?
Mince Spies!
Clare Connely

Who brings Christmas presents to dogs?
Santa paws!
Emma Kirsten

Why didn't the skeleton fall in love?
Because he didn't have the heart!
Serena Ridley

Why did Harry potter?
Because he didn't feel like rushing!
Alison Stanley

What's the most expensive sort of fish?
Goldfish!
Chanelle Taylor

What's the difference between a wizard and the letters S A M E K?
One makes spells, the other spells makes!
Amelia Churchill Blackie

What flower grows under your nose?
Tulips!
Lottie Brocklehurst

What are three ways to spread gossip?
Telephone, television, tell a friend.
Christina Evington

What goes: now you see me, now you don't,
now you see me, now you don't?
A snowman on a zebra crossing!
Meera Mistry

What's the last thing you take off when you go
to bed?
Your feet, off the floor!
Katherine Wells

What kind of cat do you find in a library?
A catalogue!
Rimal Patel

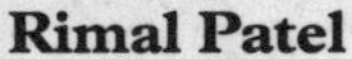

Why don't you find aspirins in the jungle?
Because the parrots-eat-'em-all'
Jessica Entwistle

What nut has no shell?
A doughnut!
Sheena Thomas

What two words have the most letters?
Post Office!
Emma Julian

Why did Captain Kirk go into the Ladies?
He wanted to go where no man had gone before!
Stacey Reid

Why did the baker stop making doughnuts?
He got fed up with the whole business!
Jilly James

What's purple and conqueror of the world?
Alexander the Grape!
Hillary Snelling

What's ten feet high
and smells?
A pig on stilts!
Stacey Reid

DINOSAUR CORNER

You'd think that dinosaurs would appear only in old jokes, but here are some new ones all sent in by **Amar Winayat** *who gets a* **NEW CHESTNUT AWARD!** *for them.*

What do you call a dinosaur with a head like a mop?
A Wipethefloorus!

What do you call a dinosaur that likes puzzles?
A Morejigsawus!

What do you call a dinosaur that lives on a beach?
A Sandyshoreus!

What do you call a sleeping dinosaur?
A Megasnorus!

What do you call a dinosaur that hides in your bedroom?
A Chestofdrawerus!

What do you call a dinosaur whose feet hurt?
A Pawsoreus!

What do you call a dinosaur that changes its mind?
A NowI'mnotsosureus!

Any more of these jokes Amar and you're goingtoboreus!

I SAY! I SAY! I SAY!

In a joke book like this, it's not what you do that's funny, it's what you say…

What did a lift that wasn't feeling very well say to the other lift?
I think I'm going down with something!
Thomas Woodhouse

What did the man say when he trod on a chocolate bar?
I've set foot on Mars!
Rimal Patel

What did one tooth say to the other tooth?
The dentist is taking me out today!
Britta Ney

What did Rudolph's wife say when the sky went black?
It looks like rain dear!
John McCaffery

What did the boy octopus say to the girl octopus?
I want to hold your hand, hand, hand, hand, hand, hand, hand, hand...
Hashern Sherif

What did one ear say to the other ear?
Between us we have brains!
Swarnjit Chohan

What did one angel say to the other angel?
Halo!
Joseph Stevenson

What did one tomato say to the other?
Go ahead and I'll ketchup!
Sara Tidey

What did ET's mother say when he came home?
Where on earth have you been?
Darren Scott

What did one flea
say to the other flea?
Shall we walk or
take the dog?
Gemma Evans

What did yellow
say to red?
We must orange
something together!
Abigail Overland

What did the big rose say to the little rose?
Hi Bud!
Hannah Masey

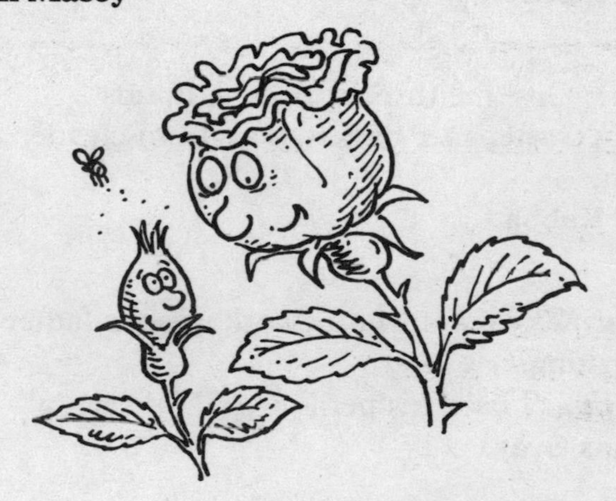

SCHOOL JOKES

Everyone knows that schools are pretty funny places. Here are some jokes to prove it!

Have you heard about the teacher who was cross-eyed?
She couldn't control her pupils!
Conor Cairns

Teacher: James, have you given the fish in the aquarium fresh water?
James: No Miss, they haven't drunk this lot yet!
Richard Bellerby

Teacher: Give me three collective nouns
Pupil: A wastepaper basket, a vacuum cleaner and a dustpan.
Namir Kubba

Teacher: Why is your homework in your father's handwriting?
Pupil: Er... I used his pen!
Nicholas Gray

Teacher: You've got your shoes on the wrong feet
Small boy: These are the only feet I've got Miss.
Robbie Burrows

Teacher: If I had forty apples in one hand, and fifty in the other, what would I have?
Pupil: Big hands!
Conor Cairns

Teacher: Give me a sentence with the word "centimetre" in it.
Pupil: My aunt was coming to stay and I was centimetre!
Conor Cairns

What do you call someone who keeps on talking when no-one is listening?
A teacher!
Grace Sivey

Teacher: Where are you from?
Pupil: Devon, Miss.
Teacher: Which part?
Pupil: All of me, Miss!
Robbie Burrows

Boy: Sir, why have you got
a sausage behind your ear?
Teacher: Oh no, I must have eaten my pencil for
lunch!
Richard Bellerby

Teacher: Write the longest sentence you can.
Pupil: Easy! "Life imprisonment."
Namir Kubba

What's the difference between a teacher and
a steam train?
One goes, "spit out that gum immediately," and the
other goes, "chew chew"!
William Dalleywater

Why did the children eat sweets in class?
Because their teachers told them not to!
James Mates

MORE ANIMALS

More jokes to prove that if you want a good laugh, go to the zoo!

What's the difference between an injured lion and a wet day?
One pours with rain, the other roars with pain.
Richard Van Neste

What is a calf called
after it's one year old?
A two-year-old calf!
Chelsea Evans

How do you communicate with fish?
Drop them a line!
Swarnjit Chohan

Why did the chicken cross the playground?
To get to the other slide!
Oliver Gale-Grant

Why don't polar bears like penguins?
They can't get the wrapper off them!
Maxine Oliver

What bird
steals cutlery?
A fork-lift
duck!
Thomas
Woodhouse

How do monkeys fly?
By King Concorde!
Subhraj Sidhu

What do birds drink out of?
Beakers!
Ashley Morrow

Where do you take a kangaroo that needs glasses?
To a hoptician!
Tom Wendland

What kind of ties do pigs wear?
Pigsties!
J Haycock

Why do bees have sticky hair?
They use honey combs!
Laura Lloyd

What happened to
the snake with a cold?
She adder viper nose!
Joseph Stevenson

What happened to Ray when he was trodden on by an elephant?
He became an X-Ray!
Chelsea Evans

What is the strongest animal?
A snail, he carries his house on his back!
Kieran Colaco

What's black and white and red all over?
A sunburnt zebra!
Michael Evans

Where would you weigh a whale?
A whale-weigh station!
Edward Emmett

What lies on its back, a hundred feet in the air?
A centipede!
Nicholas Jones

What dog keeps the best time?
A watch dog!
Katherine Wells

What's the difference between a rabbit doing exercises, and a rabbit with a flower up its nose?
One is a fit bunny, the other is a bit funny!
Joseph Cooper

What happened to the young chicken who misbehaved at school?
He was eggspelled!
Alice Lister

Mum: Don't bring that dog into the house, it's covered in fleas!
Boy: Rover, don't go into the house, it's covered in fleas!
Richard Bellerby

Why does a stork lift up one leg when it stands in water?
If it lifted up two, it would fall in!
Katherine Wells

Which came first, the chicken or the egg?
The chicken – an egg can't run!
Charlie Woollcombe-Adams

How do snails get their shells shiny?
They use snail varnish!
Samantha Rutherford

What should you put in a cat's bed to make it comfortable?
A caterpillar!
Henry Toes

What animals need oiling?
Mice!
Jenny Flynn

Why do penguins win races?
Because they're always in pole position!
Tim MacDonald-Watson

What's the safest way for a rabbit to cross a road?
Burrow under it!
Britta Ney

Which animals can jump higher than a house?
All animals; houses can't jump!
Katherine Wells

How much do penguins pay for their lunch?
Six squid!
Emma Julian

Why does the sea look friendly?
Because it's always giving little waves!
Richard Van Neste

Which animals worry
about their weight?
Fish – they always carry scales!
Thomas Yusef

DOCTOR, DOCTOR!

Going to the doctor's isn't usually very funny, unless it's in a Schoolkids' Joke Book!

What illness do retired airline pilots get?
Flu!
Charles Harrison

NEW CHESTNUT AWARD!
Why do doctors and nurses wear masks?
Because if they make a mistake you won't know who did it.
Tom Badham-Thornhill

Doctor, doctor, I can't get to sleep.
Lie on the edge of the bed, you'll soon drop off!
Charles Harrison

What's the best cure
for dandruff?
Baldness!
Dominic Floyd

Incidentally...
Why did the bald man paint
two rabbits on his head?
Because from a distance they looked like hares!
Hamish McLean

Doctor, doctor, I can see into the future.
When did this start?
Next Wednesday!
Ben Mace

Doctor, doctor, I feel like a king.
What's your name?
Joe
You must be Joe King!
Miss D Lambert

Doctor, doctor, everyone says I'm invisible.
Who said that?
Joanna Samwell

Patient: Doctor, doctor, I feel so tired, I don't know where I am half the time.
Dentist: Open wide.
Andrew Iacovides

Doctor, doctor, I keep thinking there's two of me.
One at a time please!
Constantine P.

Doctor, doctor, my nose keeps running.
Well chase it!
Jasneel Gill

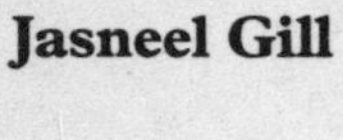

Doctor, doctor, I think I'm a marquee and a wigwam.
I see, I think you're two tents!
Abigail Nicolson

Doctor, doctor, my nose keeps running and my feet smell. What's wrong with me?
You were made upside down!
Samantha Rutherford

Doctor, doctor there's a fly in my soup.
Sorry, you're in the wrong joke!
Tom Girling

Doctor, doctor, I've just swallowed a camera.
Let's hope nothing serious develops!
Maurits Pat

Why did the orange go to the doctor?
It wasn't peeling very well.
Meg Franks

Doctor, doctor, my family thinks I'm mad.
Why?
Because I like fried eggs.
But so do I.
You do? Why don't you come and see my collection – I've got hundreds!
Andrew Garbett

✡

Doctor, doctor, how can I stop my nose running?
Stick your foot out and trip it up!
Tony Brown

WHAT'S 'ER NAME?

Who says you shouldn't call people names? Try some of these!

NEW CHESTNUT AWARD!

What do you call a vicar on a motorbike?
Rev!
Andrew Prosser

What do you call a sheep on a trampoline?
A woolly jumper!
Chris Close

What do you call a girl with tiles on her head?
Ruth! (roof – stupid!)
Nishe Selopal

What do you call a man who bounces off walls?
Rick O'Shea!
Scott McLean

What do you call a sleeping bull?
A bulldozer!
Andrew Iacovides

What do you call Batman and Robin after they've been run over by a steamroller?
Flatman and Ribbon!
Belinda Hill

What car do you keep food in?
A Larder!
Tom Hunter

What do you call a rich bear?
Winnie the Pools!
Thomas Woodhouse

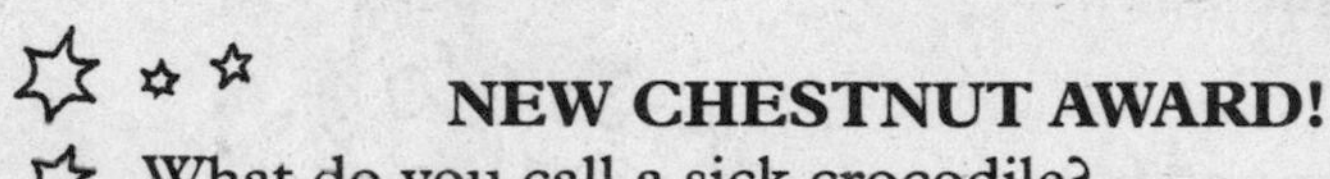

NEW CHESTNUT AWARD!

What do you call a sick crocodile?
An illogator!
Marie Shaw

What do you call a row of men waiting for a haircut?
A barberqueue!
Oliver Gill

What do you call a singing vegetable?
Tina Turnip!
Alex Leese

What do you call a woman with antlers?
Deirdre!
Jasneel Gill

What do you call Santa's wife?
Mary Christmas!
Serena Stephens

What do you call two people who embarrass you in front of your friends?
Mum and Dad!
Adam Wright

What do you call two boys with drums on their heads?
Tom, Tom!
Danielle Cooper

What do you call a girl who stands behind the goal posts?
Annette!
Rupert Griffiths

What do you call a boy who gets up your nose?
Vick!
J Haycock

What do you call a
monkey who smokes?
A chimneypanzee!
Jasneel Gill

What do you call a cat in a chemists?
Puss in Boots!
Henry Corner

What do you call someone who tells chicken jokes?
A comedi-hen!
J Haycock

What do you call an insect with six legs, that bites
and talks in code?
A morse-quito!
J Haycock

What do you call a man who can sing and drink lemonade at the same time?
A pop singer!
Thomas Spring

NEW CHESTNUT AWARD!

What do you call a fly with no wings?
A walk!
Rosemary Hurford

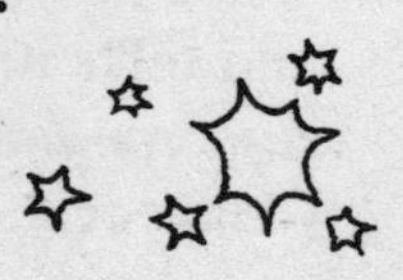

What do you call
an elephant in a
phone box?
Stuck!
Alex Leese

What do you call
a boy with his
foot in the door?
Justin!
J Haycock

What do you call a budgie run over by a lawn
mower?
Shredded Tweet!
Gemma Evans

What do you call a girl
with a frog on her head?
Lily!
Helen Boyes

POTTY POEMS!

There are few things worse than a school kid's verse!

There was an old man from Oket,
Who went for a ride in a rocket.
The rocket went bang,
His ears went twang,
And he found his nose in his pocket!
Stephanie Tucker

Little Jack Horner,
Sat in a corner,
Eating his cold meat pie.
He caught salmonella,
Poor little fella,
And now he is likely to die.
Haig Agulia

Mary had a little lamb,
It had a touch of colic.
She gave it brandy twice a day,
And now it's an alchoholic.
J Haycock

The boy stood on the burning deck,
Feeling all a-quiver.
He gave a cough,
His leg fell off,
And floated down the river!
James Hacker

Little Miss Muffet,
Sat on a tuffet,
Eating her curds and whey.
Along came a spider,
And sat down beside her,
So she squashed it.

Dachshund dog,
Crossing street,
Motor car,
Sausage meat!
Lauren Syme

OLD CHESTNUTS

Here they are – jokes that were around when your dad still had stabilisers on his bike, but are just as popular today!

Why did the one-handed man cross the road?
To get to the second-hand shop!
William Thomas

Why did the tomato blush?
Because it saw the salad dressing!
Georgie Rowe

Why did the dinosaur cross the road?
Because chickens hadn't been invented!
Antonia Brown

What did the big chimney
say to the little chimney?
You're too young
to smoke!
Kate Saller

Doctor, doctor, I keep thinking I'm a bridge.
What's come over you?
So far, three cars a bus and a lorry.
Charles Harrison

What did the policeman say to his belly button?
You're under a vest!
Adam Chen

Can I tell you a joke about butter?
I might spread it!
Rimal Patel

Why couldn't the skeleton go to the party?
He had no body to go with!
Lukas Genever

What did the traffic light say to the car?
Don't look now, I'm changing!
Meera Mistry

When is a door not a door?
When it's ajar!
Chloe Brown

Why did the hedgehog cross the road?
To see his flatmate!
Maria Westbury

Why did the boy throw his clock out of the window?
To see time fly!
Stuart Anderson

MISCELLANY OF MIRTH

A job lot of jokes, and a gaggle of giggles!

How much did the psychiatrist charge the elephant?
£15 for the appointment and £150 for the couch!
Jilly Field

Incidentally… he prescribed some trunkquillisers!

Mother: Don't you know it's rude, Billy, to keep reaching for the cake across the table. Haven't you got a tongue in your head?
Billy: Yes, Mum, but my arms are longer!
Richard Bellerby

Which footballer
laughs most?
Ryan Giggles!
Lukas Genever

Does Batman come from Cape Town?
Tommy Roberts

Why is a joker like a mushroom?
Because he's a fun guy!
Richard Van Neste

When a teddy has a toothache
what does he do?
Grin and bear it!
Gemma Leathem

Why are igloos round?
So polar bears can't hide in the corners!
Lauren McCormack

What kind of dog does a hairdresser have?
A shampoodle!
Dean Smyth

There was a man who loved trees, so he planted tall ones all over his garden.
His neighbour sued him for daylight robbery.
Andrew Ho

What happens if the Forth Bridge collapses?
We'll build a fifth one!
Thomas Yusef

How does an intruder get into a house?
Intruder window!
Tom Wendland

How does Batman's mum call him in for dinner?
Dinner dinner dinner dinner dinner dinner dinner Batman!
William Dalleywater

A man jumped off the
Empire State Building.
He wanted to make a
hit on Broadway!
Paul Arthur

A policeman was
sitting in a tree.
He was Special Branch.
Vahan Agulian

Which king invented
fractions?
Henry the $\frac{1}{8}$*th*!
Namir Kubba

A man was driving along a narrow lane when a
woman came screeching round a bend and shouted,
"Watch out pig!"
He thought this was very rude, and carried on driving.
Round the next corner he ran into a pig!
Henry Kingston

A boy walks into a pet shop and says,
"I'd like to buy a wasp please."
"We don't sell wasps," says the owner.
"Yes you do – there are two in the window,"
says the boy.
Katie Kunz

If you want to make a slow horse fast, stop feeding him!
Subhraj Sidhu

Henry and Sid were walking across the road when Sid fell down a manhole.
"Is it dark down there?" said Henry.
"I don't know, I can't see anything!" replied Sid.
Eddy Turner

A man fell down a well.
"Have you broken anything?" called down his friend.
"Of course not," replied the man, "there's nothing down here to break!"
John Franks

What do you get if you dial 48237569372647368593?
A sore finger!
Holly C.

Waiter, waiter, there's a small slug in my salad.
Sorry sir, I'll get you a bigger one!
Matthew Girling

Man on a street corner: Big Issue, Big Issue, Big Issue!
Bystander: Bless you, Bless you, Bless you!
Hashern Sherif

What's the opposite of cock-a-doodle-do?
Cock-a-doodle-don't!
Grace Sivey

Which cricket team plays half-dressed?
The Vest Indies.
Thomas Woodhouse

Did you hear about the baker who electrocuted himself?
He stood on a bun and the currant ran up his leg!
Jenny Smith

A man walked into a bar.
Ouch!
Emma Blake

Did cavemen listen to rock and roll?
Rachael Wood

Did Iron-Age people listen to heavy metal?
Jamie Tooke

What does a lion call a hunter, asleep in a hammock?
Breakfast in bed!
Mary Carroll

News flash: A man has broken into Scotland Yard and stolen all the lavatory seats.
Police say they have nothing to go on!
Joshua Stimson

Why are goldfish gold?
If they were iron, the water would turn them rusty!
Michael Ellis

What do you get if you drop a grand piano on an army base?
A flat major.
And what do you get if you drop a piano down a mineshaft?
A flat miner.
Eve Harris

✡

What animal do you most resemble
when you have a bath?
A Bear!
Rimal Patel

What is worse than finding a maggot in your apple?
Finding half a maggot!
Debbie Brogden

Did you hear about the man who drowned in a bowl of muesli?
He was pulled under by a strong currant...
Jim Girling

"Did you share your sledge nicely with your little brother?" asked Mum.
"Yes," said Freddie, "I had it going downhill and he had it going uphill."
Andrew Ho

"My career is in ruins."
"I'm sorry to hear that."
"There's no need to be, I'm an archaeologist!"
Robbie Burrows

A boy asked his mum what she was cooking.
"It's bean soup," said his mum.
"I don't care what it's been, what is it now?" said the boy.
David Jenkins

Did you hear about the boy who was named after his father?
They called him "Dad"!
Jimmy Flint

Did you hear about the footballer who turned up for a match wearing his wife's perfume?
He was scent off!
Amar Winayat

Thanks to all these *Readathon* schools for sending in the jokes:

School	Town
Coventry Preparatory School	Coventry
The Lindens	Stroud
Houghton School	Huntingdon
St George's School	Jersey
Hazlegrove House	Yeovil
Lickey Hill First and Middle School	Rednal
Ruislip Gardens School	Ruislip
The Mall School	Twickenham
St Leonard's-Mayfield School	Mayfield
Frideswide Middle School	Oxford
Landulph School	Plymouth
St Margaret's School	Liverpool
Leeds Girls' High School	Leeds
Badger Hill Primary School	York
Clifton High Lower School	Bristol
Donegall Road Primary School	Belfast
St Aidan's Primary	Wishaw
Beaudesert Park School	Stroud

With apologies to anyone whose name appears incorrectly spelled – reading hundreds of handwritten jokes was no laughing matter!

THE SCHOOLKIDS' JOKE BOOK

Compiled by Brough Girling

How do you make a band stand?
Hide all their chairs!

What do you get if you sit under a cow?
A pat on the head!

There are hundreds more like these in this hilarious collection of jokes supplied by school children throughout the country.

0 00 692861 7
£3.50

Compiled by Brough Girling

Guess what can be right but never wrong?
A right-angled triangle!

What's the difference between the Spice Girls and Pavarotti?
Their weight!

Check out more howlers in this crazy collection of jokes supplied by schoolkids throughout the country – are you loopy enough to read it?

0 00 694585 6
£3.50